First published by Parragon in 2007

Parragon
Queen Street House
4 Queen Street
Bath BA1 1HE, UK

Copyright © Parragon Books Ltd 2007

All rights reserved. No part of this publication may be reproduced, stored in a retrieval system, or transmitted by any means, mechanical, photocopying, recording, or otherwise, without the prior permission of the copyright holder.

ISBN 978-1-4054-9567-7
Printed in China

Little Kitten Finds the Moon

Illustrated by Sophie Groves   Written by Kath Jewitt

Bath · New York · Singapore · Hong Kong · Cologne · Delhi · Melbourne

One evening Charlie the kitten was playing in the backyard.
"It's time for bed," called his mommy.
But Charlie didn't hear her.
He was too busy chasing fireflies.

Suddenly Charlie found himself on the street. He had never been out there before, and it was getting dark. Charlie felt a little bit afraid.

Then he remembered something his mommy had said.

"All cats have special eyes to see in the dark," he told himself.

"So there's no need to be scared."

Charlie saw a bright light. The light got bigger and bigger, and brighter and brighter. "What's that?" he wondered.

BEEP! went a car horn. "Oh my!" gasped Charlie, leaping on to a wall. "I didn't know cars had special eyes, too!"

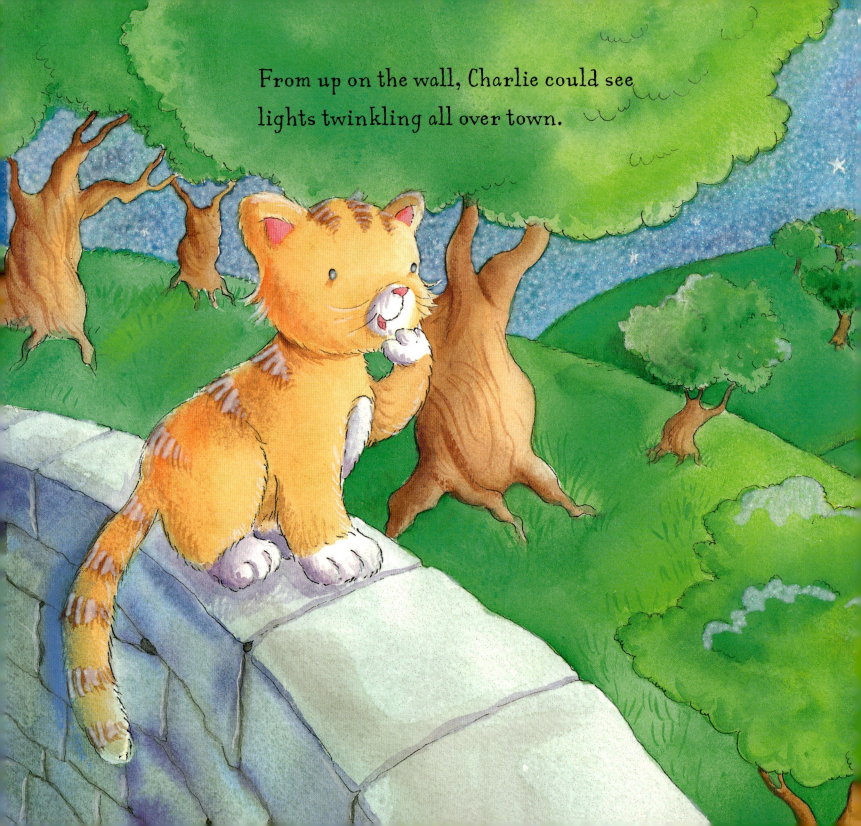
From up on the wall, Charlie could see lights twinkling all over town.

"The world looks beautiful at night," he thought. He sat and watched the shining lights for a long time.

While Charlie watched, the lights started to go out as everyone went to bed. Soon, all the houses were in darkness, but something was still shining.

Charlie looked up and saw a big silver ball in the branches of a tree. It was shining over the whole town.

"What a beautiful ball," thought Charlie. He climbed the tree to take a closer look. But the branches were empty, except for a little fluffy squirrel.

"Do you know where the ball has gone?" Charlie asked.

"It's up there," replied the squirrel. She pointed to the roof of a house.

"I'll climb up and fetch it," Charlie said. "Then we can play ball together, if you want."

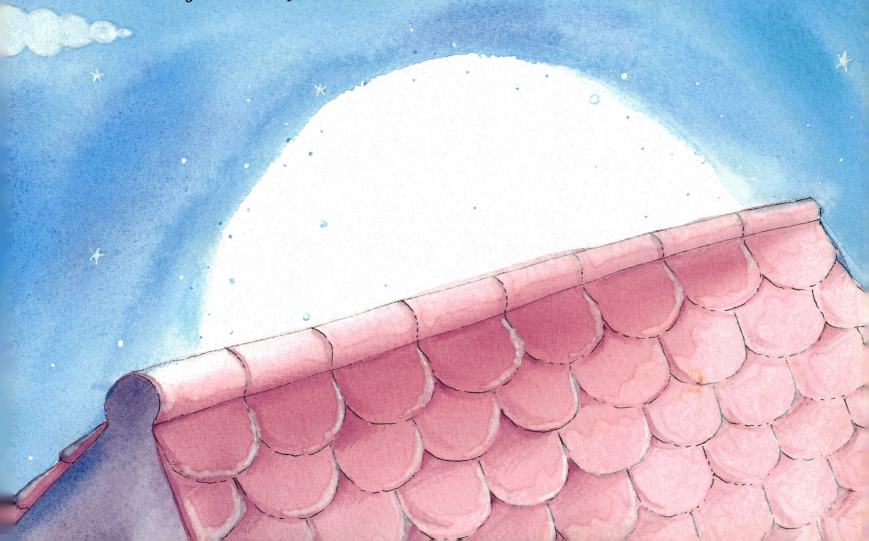

But when Charlie climbed onto the roof, the ball had gone again. Now it was shining up in the sky. Charlie looked down at the ground. It was a VERY long way down. He wished he had never come out on to the street or climbed so high. He knew that he wasn't being good. "I want to go home," he meowed.

"Then come along with me," said a gentle voice. It was Charlie's mommy. She had come to find him.

"You shouldn't be out here on your own, Charlie," she told him.

"There's a silver ball in the sky. Can I take it home?" Charlie asked. His mother smiled. "That's not a ball," she said. "It's the Moon. Sometimes it looks so big and bright, you think you can touch it. But it lives high in the sky. Even the birds can't reach it."

"What's it for?" yawned Charlie.

"To light up the dark," replied his mother, "and to watch over us while we sleep. Come on, sleepy head. It's time for bed."